"MASTERING REFLECTIVE TEACHING: ELEVATING PROFESSIONALISM AND PEDAGOGICAL SKILLS"

SANJANA MISHRA

Made with ♥ on the Notion Press Platform
www.notionpress.com

Dedicated to

With heartfelt gratitude, I dedicate this work to Rahul College of Education, an institution that has been a beacon of light in shaping the future of education. Your unwavering commitment to nurturing teachers with integrity, compassion, and a profound understanding of pedagogy has inspired countless individuals, myself included.

To the leadership, faculty, and staff, thank you for your dedication to fostering a nurturing and enriching environment where educators are empowered to lead, innovate, and inspire. Your tireless efforts have cultivated not only knowledge but also the values that are critical to shaping future generations.

This dedication stands as a tribute to your excellence, resilience, and unrelenting pursuit of educational advancement. May your influence continue to uplift and guide all those who pass through your halls.

Contents

Foreword

"To teach is to learn twice over; reflecting on teaching is the secret to unlocking professional growth." – Joseph Joubert

In the rapidly evolving world of education, the importance of reflective teaching cannot be overstated. As educators, we are continually tasked with not only delivering knowledge but also refining our methods, adapting to diverse learner needs, and responding to the challenges of a dynamic classroom environment. Mastering Reflective Teaching: Elevating Professionalism and Pedagogical Skills is a timely and comprehensive guide that addresses these demands by championing the practice of reflective teaching as a cornerstone of professional growth.

Reflective teaching offers educators an invaluable opportunity to examine their teaching practices, question their assumptions, and continuously improve. It fosters a mindset of lifelong learning, which is essential for navigating the complexities of modern education. This book eloquently illustrates the power of self-reflection in helping teachers move beyond rote methodologies to cultivate a deeper, more responsive engagement with their students.

Through this text, readers will embark on a journey that underscores the importance of understanding one's instructional choices, analyzing student feedback, and engaging with pedagogical research. Whether you are an aspiring teacher, a seasoned educator, or a professional development leader, the strategies outlined in this book will prove indispensable in enhancing the quality of education delivered in your classrooms.

It is rare to come across a resource that so effectively blends theoretical insights with practical applications. The case studies, reflective exercises, and evidence-based techniques contained within these pages serve as a roadmap for teachers striving to elevate their craft. More importantly, the book encourages educators to view reflection not as an occasional practice, but as an ongoing commitment to their own professional journey.

I commend the authors for their dedication to producing a work that will undoubtedly shape the future of teaching. Their expertise and passion for education shine through every chapter, making Mastering Reflective Teaching not just a tool for development, but an inspirational call to embrace the evolving nature of the teaching profession.

May this book inspire you to reflect, grow, and continue making a profound impact on the lives of your students.

Preface

"The heart of reflective teaching is asking the question: How can I improve?" – Charlotte Danielson

In an era where education is rapidly evolving, the role of a teacher is no longer confined to the mere dissemination of knowledge. Today, educators are required to navigate complex classrooms, cater to diverse learning needs, and continuously enhance their professional and pedagogical skills. Reflective teaching, therefore, emerges as a powerful tool in this dynamic landscape, allowing educators to critically assess their teaching practices and strive for excellence.

Mastering Reflective Teaching: Elevating Professionalism and Pedagogical Skills is a comprehensive guide for educators committed to developing a reflective mindset. It is designed to provide insights into the importance of reflection in teaching and how it contributes to the overall professional development of an educator. By reflecting on their teaching strategies, classroom interactions, and learning outcomes, teachers can identify areas for improvement, foster better student engagement, and elevate the overall learning experience.

This book draws on both theoretical frameworks and practical examples to guide teachers through the process of reflective practice. Each chapter is thoughtfully crafted to address the various facets of teaching that require reflection—from lesson planning to classroom management, and from student assessment to self-evaluation. Furthermore, it emphasizes the role of reflective teaching in fostering an educator's professional identity, encouraging lifelong learning, and promoting a deeper connection between theory and practice.

My own journey as an educator has been profoundly shaped by reflective practices. Over the years, I have come to realize that it is not just about what we teach, but how we teach, and more importantly, how we learn from our teaching experiences. Through reflection, we can become more self-aware, more adaptable, and more attuned to the needs of our students.

It is my hope that this book will serve as a valuable resource for both new and experienced educators who are eager to enhance their professional growth. By mastering reflective teaching, we can collectively contribute to a more enriching and effective educational environment—one that nurtures both students and educators alike.

I invite you to embark on this reflective journey, and I trust that the insights shared in these pages will inspire you to elevate your professionalism and pedagogical skills.

Acknowledgements

"Education is not the filling of a pail, but the lighting of a fire."

— William Butler Yeats

I would like to express my deepest gratitude to everyone who has contributed to the creation of this book.

I extend my heartfelt thanks to **Shri Lallan R. Tiwari, Chairman of Rahul Education**, for his remarkable vision and leadership in shaping the educational landscape. His unwavering dedication and passion for education have not only fostered an environment of academic excellence but have also laid a solid foundation for countless students and educators to thrive.

Under his guidance, **Rahul Education has consistently upheld its commitment to providing quality education, nurturing future leaders, and promoting holistic development. Shri Lallan R. Tiwari's** forward-thinking approach and continuous support have played an instrumental role in advancing the mission of Rahul Education, empowering the institution to reach greater heights.

The **values of integrity, perseverance, and a relentless pursuit of knowledge that Shri Tiwari exemplifies serve as a source of inspiration for all of us.** His contributions to the educational sector are both significant and deeply appreciated. I am truly grateful for his efforts in creating an institution that continues to shape and mold individuals who will make meaningful contributions to society.

In conclusion, I express **my deepest gratitude to Shri Lallan R. Tiwari for his enduring commitment to education and for the impact he has made on the lives of many through Rahul Education.**

Prologue

Prologue

In the ever-evolving landscape of education, the role of the teacher is continuously transforming. No longer is the educator merely a transmitter of knowledge, but rather a guide, facilitator, and lifelong learner. The rapid pace of technological advancement, shifting educational paradigms, and the growing diversity in classrooms demand that teachers are more adaptive, reflective, and professional in their approach.

Mastering Reflective Teaching: Elevating Professionalism and Pedagogical Skills is born from the recognition that effective teaching today requires more than a sound knowledge base and good intentions. It demands conscious self-examination, an ongoing commitment to improvement, and the capacity to rethink and reshape pedagogical practices. Reflective teaching is not just a process, but a mindset—a commitment to critical introspection, inquiry, and action that fosters both personal and professional growth.

This book seeks to illuminate the path toward reflective practice, offering educators the tools, strategies, and frameworks to not only enhance their own teaching skills but also to contribute to a greater culture of professionalism in education. Each chapter builds upon key principles of reflection, providing actionable insights and fostering a deeper understanding of one's own teaching philosophy.

At its core, reflective teaching emphasizes the importance of learning from one's experiences, adapting to new challenges, and staying attuned to the unique needs of students. It celebrates the journey of continual growth—a path that begins with a single, critical question: *How can I become a better educator for the sake of my students and my own professional fulfillment?*

As you embark on this reflective journey through the pages of this book, I invite you to not only engage with its concepts but to make them your own. Let this be the catalyst that elevates your teaching practice, helping you to become not just a teacher, but a reflective educator—one who is committed to mastering their craft and shaping the future of education.

ONE

Chapter 1: Introduction to Reflective Teaching

"We do not learn from experience... we learn from reflecting on experience." John Dewey

Reflective teaching is a process where teachers think about their teaching practices, analyze their effectiveness, and make necessary adjustments for improvement. It is a critical part of professional development, encouraging educators to continuously evaluate their approaches in order to enhance student learning outcomes. This chapter explores key concepts in reflective teaching, explains why teachers should engage in reflective practices, provides an overview of different types of reflection, and highlights the profound impact reflective teaching has on professional growth.

Key Concepts: Definition and Significance of Reflective Teaching

Reflective teaching refers to the systematic process by which educators critically assess their teaching methodologies, decisions, and interactions with students to foster improvement. Originating from John Dewey's theories on reflective thought, reflective teaching is seen as an essential component of experiential learning. Dewey emphasized the importance of active, persistent, and careful consideration of beliefs, practices, and their consequences, which mirrors the reflective process teachers undergo.

The significance of reflective teaching lies in its ability to empower educators to become lifelong learners, constantly refining their craft. It moves beyond the passive acceptance of routine practices and encourages a dynamic, iterative approach to teaching. Teachers engage in self-examination, identifying strengths, weaknesses, and areas for development. Through this continuous process, they ensure that their teaching remains relevant, responsive to students' needs, and informed by the latest pedagogical theories and evidence.

In an era where the educational landscape is rapidly evolving due to technological advancements, shifting student demographics, and new learning paradigms, reflective teaching ensures that educators are adaptive and resilient. It fosters an environment of active professional engagement, where teachers are agents of change, continually enhancing their skills and contributing to the collective knowledge base of the teaching profession.

Objectives: Why Teachers Should Engage in Reflective Practices

Engaging in reflective teaching has several objectives, each of which contributes to the improvement of educational practices and student learning. Reflective teaching encourages educators to become more aware of their own beliefs, values, and assumptions about teaching and learning. This self-awareness helps them align their actions with their educational philosophy, ensuring consistency between what they believe about teaching and how they enact those beliefs in the classroom.

Enhanced Instructional Effectiveness

Reflective practice helps teachers refine their instructional strategies to meet the diverse needs of students. By examining which methods are most effective, educators can adapt their techniques to cater to different learning styles and abilities. Reflection allows teachers to assess whether their teaching objectives are being met and, if not, to adjust their approach accordingly.

Increased Responsiveness to Student Needs

Through reflective practices, teachers become more attuned to the challenges and obstacles their students face. By identifying areas where students struggle, teachers can adjust their methods, offering more targeted support, differentiation, and individualized instruction. Reflection encourages educators to recognize that student learning is complex and multifaceted, requiring a nuanced approach to teaching.

Promoting Lifelong Learning and Professional Development

Reflective teaching fosters a culture of continuous learning, not only for students but for teachers as well. Engaging in reflection encourages teachers to stay updated with the latest research, trends, and educational innovations. This ongoing professional development is vital in a field where new methodologies and technologies are constantly emerging.

Fostering Collaboration and Collegiality

Reflective practices often lead to collaborative learning communities within schools. Teachers who reflect on their teaching are more likely to share their insights and strategies with colleagues, fostering an environment of collegiality and support. This collaboration benefits both teachers and students, as it creates a collective pool of knowledge and resources.

Improved Student Outcomes

Ultimately, the goal of reflective teaching is to improve student outcomes. By continuously assessing and refining their teaching practices, educators create more effective learning environments that promote higher levels of student achievement. Reflection helps teachers identify strategies that work and eliminate those that do not, leading to better instructional practices and, consequently, better student performance.

Overview of Reflection Types: Technical, Practical, and Critical Reflection

Reflective teaching encompasses several types of reflection, each serving a unique purpose in the teaching-learning process. Three primary types of reflection—technical, practical, and critical—are integral to comprehensive reflective practice.

TechnicalReflection

Technical reflection is focused on the efficiency and effectiveness of teaching methods. It involves analyzing the use of specific strategies and techniques in relation to pre-set goals. Teachers engaging in technical reflection ask questions like, "Did the lesson meet its objectives?" or "Did the students understand the material?" This type of reflection is often concerned with immediate classroom outcomes and seeks to refine the practical aspects of teaching, such as lesson planning, classroom management, and assessment techniques.

While important, technical reflection alone may be insufficient, as it tends to focus primarily on what teachers do, rather than why they do it. It is often limited to problem-solving and surface-level adjustments without addressing underlying pedagogical beliefs.

PracticalReflection

Practical reflection delves deeper, focusing on the relationship between the teacher's actions and the broader learning goals. It goes beyond the immediate concerns of technical reflection to examine the values, principles, and purposes behind teaching practices. Teachers engaging in practical reflection consider questions like, "Why did I choose this particular teaching strategy?" or "How does this activity align with my educational philosophy?"

Practical reflection allows educators to consider the broader implications of their actions and the extent to which their teaching aligns with their overall goals for student development. This type of reflection encourages educators to think about the impact of their teaching on student engagement, motivation, and long-term learning outcomes.

Critical Reflection

Critical reflection moves beyond the technical and practical aspects of teaching to question the social, cultural, and ethical dimensions of education. It asks teachers to consider how their teaching practices are influenced by broader societal norms, power structures, and inequities. Critical reflection prompts educators to question assumptions about knowledge, teaching, and learning, particularly those related to issues of equity, inclusion, and social justice.

For example, a critically reflective teacher might ask, "Whose voices are being privileged in my curriculum?" or "How can I create a more inclusive and equitable classroom environment?" Critical reflection is vital in fostering a more socially responsible and inclusive education system. It encourages teachers to recognize and challenge biases, both within themselves and within the educational system, and to advocate for practices that promote equity and social justice.

Impact on Professional Growth

Reflective teaching plays a crucial role in the professional growth of educators. By engaging in regular reflection, teachers develop a deeper understanding of their own practice, leading to greater self-awareness and a clearer sense of purpose. Reflective practice encourages teachers to move from being reactive to proactive, taking ownership of their professional development and continually seeking ways to improve.

Developing a Growth Mindset

Reflection fosters a growth mindset, where teachers view challenges and setbacks as opportunities for learning rather than as failures. By embracing reflection, teachers develop resilience and adaptability, qualities that are essential in a constantly evolving educational landscape. This mindset enables teachers to approach their professional development with curiosity and openness, rather than with fear or resistance.

Promoting Self-Regulation and Autonomy

Reflective practice encourages teachers to become more self-regulated learners. Rather than relying solely on external feedback, reflective teachers take an active role in assessing their own performance and identifying areas for improvement. This autonomy empowers teachers to take charge of their own learning and to pursue professional development opportunities that align with their individual goals and needs.

Encouraging Lifelong Learning

Reflective teaching fosters a culture of lifelong learning. Teachers who engage in reflection are more likely to seek out professional development opportunities, collaborate with colleagues, and stay informed about new research and trends in education. This commitment to ongoing learning not only benefits teachers but also has a positive impact on students, as it leads to more innovative and effective teaching practices.

Building Professional Resilience

The challenges of teaching can often lead to burnout, especially when teachers feel overwhelmed by the demands of the profession. Reflective practice helps teachers build professional resilience by providing them with the tools to navigate challenges and setbacks. Through reflection, teachers can gain new perspectives, develop problem-solving skills, and cultivate a sense of agency in their work.

Contributing to a Culture of Collaboration

Finally, reflective practice encourages a collaborative approach to professional growth. Teachers who engage in reflection are more likely to share their insights and experiences with colleagues, creating a culture of collaboration and mutual support. This collaboration not only enhances individual professional growth but also contributes to the overall improvement of the educational system.

Conclusion

Reflective teaching is an indispensable tool for professional growth and development. It empowers teachers to critically evaluate their practice, make informed decisions, and continuously improve their effectiveness in the classroom. By engaging in technical, practical, and critical reflection, educators can ensure that their teaching is not only effective but also aligned with their values and responsive to the needs of all students. Ultimately, reflective teaching fosters a dynamic, responsive, and inclusive educational environment that promotes both teacher and student success.

TWO

CHAPTER 2: HISTORICAL CONTEXT AND EVOLUTION OF REFLECTIVE TEACHING

"Teaching is above all a critically reflective practice."Stephen Brookfield:

Reflective teaching is an approach to education that encourages educators to critically analyze and evaluate their teaching practices to enhance professional growth. Its historical roots trace back centuries, evolving in response to shifting educational philosophies, societal changes, and psychological research. This chapter explores the development of reflective teaching, from its early conceptualizations to its present-day applications, and considers its evolution in relation to key educational movements and thinkers.

Early Foundations of Reflective Thought in Education

Reflective teaching draws on the broader concept of reflection, which has its philosophical underpinnings in ancient Greece. Socrates, one of the earliest proponents of reflection, used dialectic methods to encourage self-examination, famously coining the phrase, "The unexamined life is not worth living." This focus on self-awareness and critical thinking forms the philosophical foundation of reflective teaching.

Later, during the Enlightenment period, philosophers like John Locke and Jean-Jacques Rousseau advanced the notion of experiential learning, which is closely tied to reflection. Locke's Tabula Rasa emphasized that knowledge is derived from sensory experiences, and Rousseau's Emile advocated for a naturalistic education where children learn through experience and reflection. These ideas laid the groundwork for educators to consider the impact of their teaching methods and the experiences they create for learners.

The Influence of John Dewey and Pragmatism

The formalization of reflective teaching as an educational practice is largely attributed to the American philosopher and educator John Dewey in the early 20th century. Dewey, a leading figure in the progressive education movement, introduced the concept of reflection as a crucial component of the learning process. In his seminal work, "How We Think" (1910), Dewey described reflective thinking as an active, persistent, and careful consideration of any belief or supposed form of knowledge in light of the grounds that support it and the further conclusions to which it tends.

Dewey argued that effective teaching requires educators to be reflective practitioners who constantly assess and adjust their methods based on student outcomes. His theory of experiential learning emphasized the importance of reflection in fostering intellectual growth and problem-solving abilities. Dewey's ideas greatly influenced teacher education programs, encouraging teachers to view themselves as lifelong learners and reflective thinkers.

Post-World War II Educational Reforms and the Rise of Reflective Teaching

The post-World War II era saw significant changes in education worldwide, as nations sought to rebuild and modernize their educational systems. In the United States and Europe, there was a growing emphasis on teacher professionalism and the importance of teacher training. This period saw the emergence of educational psychology as a distinct discipline, with researchers like Jean Piaget and Lev Vygotsky exploring cognitive development and social learning theories. Their work reinforced the notion that learning is an active, reflective process, not a passive reception of information.

In the 1970s and 1980s, reflective teaching gained prominence through the work of scholars like Donald Schön, who introduced the concept of the "reflective practitioner" in his influential book "The Reflective Practitioner: How Professionals Think in Action" (1983). Schön argued that professionals, including teachers, should engage in "reflection-in-action" (reflecting while teaching) and "reflection-on-action" (reflecting after teaching) to continually improve their practices. This marked a shift from the traditional, top-down approach to teaching, where educators were seen as passive transmitters of knowledge, to one where teachers were encouraged to be active participants in their professional development.

The Growth of Action Research and Teacher as Researcher Movements

The 1980s and 1990s saw the growth of action research, a participatory research method that involves teachers systematically investigating their practices to improve teaching and learning. This movement empowered educators to take control of their professional development and placed reflection at the heart of the process. Action research encourages teachers to identify problems in their classrooms, develop strategies to address them, implement those strategies, and reflect on the outcomes.

The "teacher as researcher" movement paralleled the rise of action research, emphasizing that teachers should not just be passive recipients of educational theory but active contributors to the field of educational research. Reflective teaching became central to this movement, as teachers engaged in systematic reflection to better understand their students' needs, adapt their instructional methods, and contribute to the broader body of educational knowledge.

Reflective Teaching in the 21st Century

Reflective teaching in the 21st century continues to evolve in response to new educational challenges and technological advancements. The global shift towards learner-centered pedagogy, which prioritizes student engagement and active learning, aligns closely with reflective teaching practices. Teachers are encouraged to constantly adapt their methods based on classroom feedback, student performance, and emerging educational technologies.

The integration of digital tools in education has expanded the possibilities for reflective teaching. Online teaching platforms, digital portfolios, and video analysis tools provide new avenues for teachers to engage in self-reflection and peer feedback. These technologies allow educators to record their lessons, analyze their teaching practices, and collaborate with colleagues in reflective communities, even across geographic boundaries.

Moreover, global educational movements such as inclusive education and culturally responsive teaching have highlighted the need for teachers to reflect on their biases, assumptions, and cultural competencies. Reflective teaching has become a tool for promoting equity and inclusion in classrooms, as educators critically examine how their instructional methods impact diverse student populations and make necessary adjustments to create more inclusive learning environments.

Critiques and Challenges of Reflective Teaching

Despite its widespread adoption, reflective teaching is not without its critiques and challenges. One of the main criticisms is that reflection can be time-consuming, particularly in education systems where teachers are already burdened with heavy workloads. Some educators may find it difficult to allocate the time necessary for deep reflection, especially if they lack institutional support or resources.

Another challenge is that reflective teaching requires a high degree of self-awareness and openness to change, which may be difficult for some teachers to develop. Resistance to change, fear of criticism, or a lack of reflective skills can hinder the effectiveness of reflective teaching practices. Furthermore, there is a risk that reflection, if not guided by clear objectives or frameworks, can become superficial or self-congratulatory rather than genuinely transformative.

To address these challenges, teacher education programs and professional development initiatives must provide structured opportunities for reflection, clear frameworks for reflective practice, and support systems to help teachers engage meaningfully in reflective processes.

The Future of Reflective Teaching

Looking ahead, the future of reflective teaching is likely to be shaped by ongoing developments in educational research, technology, and societal changes. As classrooms become more diverse and educational expectations continue to rise, reflective teaching will remain an essential tool for educators to adapt to the evolving needs of students.

One promising trend is the increasing emphasis on collaborative reflection, where teachers work together in professional learning communities to reflect on their practices, share insights, and develop new strategies. Collaborative reflection fosters a culture of continuous improvement and supports educators in navigating the complexities of modern teaching.

Additionally, the growing focus on social-emotional learning (SEL) and mental health in education underscores the importance of reflective teaching in addressing the holistic needs of students. Teachers who reflect on their emotional responses, classroom dynamics, and relationships with students are better equipped to create supportive, emotionally safe learning environments.

Conclusion

Reflective teaching has evolved from philosophical traditions of self-examination to become a cornerstone of modern educational practice. From the contributions of John Dewey and Donald Schön to the rise of action research and the integration of digital tools, reflective teaching has transformed how educators approach their professional growth and classroom practices. While challenges remain, particularly in terms of time and resources, the future of reflective teaching is bright, with new opportunities for collaboration, technology integration, and a deeper focus on student well-being. As education continues to evolve, reflective teaching will remain a critical practice for fostering effective, adaptive, and compassionate educators.

THREE

Chapter 3: Reflective Teaching and Professionalism

"The reflective practitioner thinks critically about the practice, striving for continuous improvement.":Donald Schön

Reflective teaching and professionalism are two key pillars in modern education, contributing to the evolution of teachers and improving student outcomes. Reflective teaching involves a continual process where educators critically assess their teaching practices and make informed adjustments to enhance learning. Professionalism, in this context, refers to the qualities, behaviors, and ethics that teachers uphold to maintain a high standard in their profession. This essay delves into the relationship between reflective teaching and professionalism, exploring their significance, strategies, and their impact on the educational environment.

Understanding Reflective Teaching

Reflective teaching can be defined as a conscious effort by educators to assess, analyze, and refine their instructional practices.

It is rooted in the idea that teaching is not a static profession but one that evolves through experience and critical self-examination. Reflection enables teachers to become aware of what works and what does not in their classrooms, allowing them to make data-informed decisions that benefit their students.

Reflective teaching is often guided by the following principles:

Self-awareness: Teachers must be aware of their own teaching style, strengths, and weaknesses.

Critical thinking: Educators should critically assess their instructional methods and their impact on student engagement and achievement.

Continuous improvement: Reflection encourages a growth mindset, where teachers are always striving for better outcomes through experimentation and adaptation.

This concept can be traced back to John Dewey's work on experiential learning. Dewey believed that reflection bridges the gap between theory and practice, allowing educators to draw meaningful insights from their teaching experiences. Through reflection, teachers move beyond routine teaching and become active participants in their own professional growth.

Methods of Reflective Teaching

There are several methods teachers can employ to incorporate reflective practice into their teaching routine. These include:

Journaling: Writing reflective journals after lessons can help teachers document their thoughts, feelings, and observations about the class. This written record can be reviewed periodically to identify trends and areas for improvement.

Peer Observation: Collaborating with colleagues and participating in peer observation allows teachers to receive constructive feedback from others. This external perspective can shed light on areas that may not be apparent to the teacher.

Self-assessment: Teachers can use self-assessment tools to evaluate their teaching methods. These can include student feedback, performance data, or video recordings of lessons.

Action Research: Reflective teaching can also take the form of small-scale action research, where teachers identify a problem or area for improvement, implement a solution, and assess the results. This cycle of inquiry helps in refining teaching strategies over time.

Incorporating reflective practices not only improves teaching effectiveness but also helps educators remain responsive to the diverse needs of students. By continuously reflecting, teachers become more adaptable, creative, and empathetic.

Professionalism in Teaching

Professionalism in teaching goes beyond mere competence. It involves a deep commitment to ethical standards, continuous learning, and fostering positive relationships with students, colleagues, and the community. Professionalism is essential for creating an environment of trust and respect, where students feel supported and valued.

The core elements of professionalism in teaching include:

Ethical Responsibility: Teachers are often seen as role models, and their behavior sets an example for students. Professionalism requires educators to uphold high ethical standards in their conduct, ensuring fairness, inclusivity, and respect in the classroom.

Lifelong Learning: Education is a rapidly changing field, and teachers must commit to lifelong learning to stay current with new teaching strategies, technologies, and educational research. Professional development workshops, seminars, and courses help teachers stay updated and bring fresh insights into their practice.

Collaboration: Professionalism also involves working collaboratively with colleagues, students, and parents. Effective communication and teamwork foster a healthy school culture and support student success.

Accountability: Teachers are accountable not only for the academic performance of their students but also for their own actions and decisions. Being professional means being reflective and open to constructive criticism, always seeking to improve one's teaching methods.

The Relationship Between Reflective Teaching and Professionalism

Reflective teaching and professionalism are deeply interconnected. Reflection is a key component of professionalism because it requires teachers to continually evaluate and refine their practices. In turn, professionalism demands that teachers engage in reflective practices to ensure that their teaching aligns with ethical and educational standards.

Self-improvement: Both reflective teaching and professionalism are driven by the goal of self-improvement. Reflective teachers assess their performance regularly, identifying areas for growth, while professionalism compels them to seek out opportunities for development and stay informed about new pedagogical trends.

Ethical Awareness: Reflection encourages teachers to consider the ethical dimensions of their actions. By reflecting on their interactions with students and their instructional decisions, teachers can ensure that they are promoting fairness, equity, and respect in the classroom.

Adaptability: Reflective teaching fosters adaptability, a key trait of professionalism. As teachers reflect on their practice, they become more aware of the diverse needs of their students and can adjust their teaching methods accordingly. This flexibility is vital in maintaining a professional approach to education, where the focus is always on student learning.

Challenges of Reflective Teaching and Professionalism

While the benefits of reflective teaching and professionalism are numerous, there are also challenges. These include:

Time Constraints: Teachers often face heavy workloads, leaving little time for reflection. Incorporating reflective practices into a busy schedule requires strong time-management skills and a commitment to prioritizing professional growth.

Emotional Labor: Reflecting on one's teaching can be an emotionally charged process, particularly when confronting difficult situations or failures. Teachers must be resilient and willing to engage in honest self-evaluation.

Institutional Support: For reflective teaching to thrive, schools and educational institutions need to provide adequate support. This includes offering professional development opportunities, creating a culture of collaboration, and encouraging open dialogue among educators.

Maintaining Motivation: Teachers may sometimes struggle to maintain their motivation for reflection and professional development, especially in challenging environments. It is important for educators to find intrinsic motivation and seek external support, such as mentorship or peer groups, to sustain their commitment to growth.

Impact of Reflective Teaching and Professionalism on Student Learning

Ultimately, reflective teaching and professionalism have a profound impact on student learning. When teachers are reflective and professional, they create a more engaging and inclusive learning environment that fosters student success. Reflective teachers are better equipped to understand the unique needs of their students and tailor their instruction to meet those needs, leading to improved academic outcomes.

Professionalism also ensures that teachers maintain a high standard of ethical conduct and model positive behaviors for their students. This not only enhances the learning experience but also helps students develop important social and emotional skills, such as empathy, responsibility, and respect for others.

Conclusion

Reflective teaching and professionalism are essential components of effective teaching. By engaging in reflective practices, teachers continuously improve their instructional methods and respond to the evolving needs of their students. Professionalism, on the other hand, ensures that teachers maintain high ethical standards, stay committed to lifelong learning, and collaborate effectively with others.

Together, these practices contribute to a positive and dynamic learning environment where both teachers and students can thrive.

Despite the challenges that may arise, the benefits of reflective teaching and professionalism are undeniable, making them indispensable to the teaching profession. As education continues to evolve, the integration of these concepts will remain crucial to the development of skilled, compassionate, and innovative educators.

FOUR

Chapter 4: Techniques and Strategies for Reflective Teaching

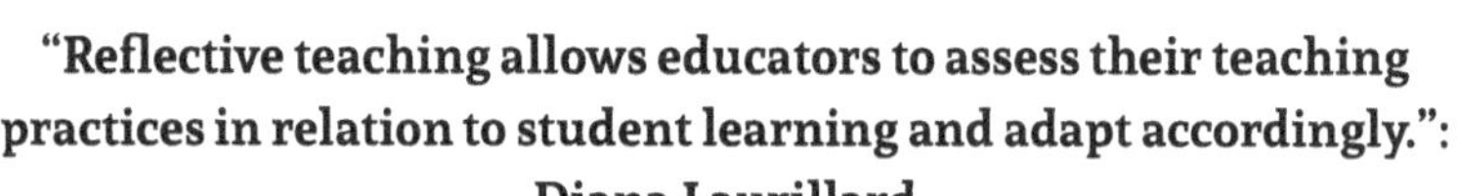

"Reflective teaching allows educators to assess their teaching practices in relation to student learning and adapt accordingly.": Diana Laurillard

Reflective teaching is a powerful process that allows educators to critically analyze their practices and continuously evolve to meet the diverse needs of learners. It moves beyond the traditional, rigid methods of instruction by encouraging self-awareness, adaptability, and informed decision-making. Reflective teaching, when practiced regularly, fosters a classroom environment that is dynamic and responsive to student engagement, ultimately leading to more effective pedagogy. This essay explores the essential techniques and strategies for reflective teaching, the benefits it provides for educators and students, and practical ways to incorporate it into daily educational practices.

Understanding Reflective Teaching

Reflective teaching is grounded in the idea that teachers must constantly evaluate their own practices, beliefs, and classroom interactions. According to Dewey's theory of reflection, teachers who engage in reflective thinking can develop a deeper understanding of their teaching strategies and improve them. The process involves questioning not only what happens in the classroom but also why it happens, thereby promoting professional growth. Reflection requires a cyclical approach where teachers plan, act, observe, and reflect on their actions.

Key Techniques for Reflective Teaching

Effective reflective teaching involves the adoption of various techniques that guide teachers through their reflective journey:

a. Keeping a Reflective Journal

One of the simplest and most effective ways to begin reflective teaching is by keeping a reflective journal. Teachers can use this journal to document classroom experiences, teaching methods, challenges, and breakthroughs. Regular entries encourage educators to analyze specific classroom situations and assess what worked, what didn't, and why. The act of writing fosters self-awareness and promotes critical thinking, allowing educators to identify patterns or recurring issues that may need to be addressed.

b. Peer Observation and Feedback

Collaboration with colleagues through peer observation is another valuable technique for reflective teaching. By inviting fellow teachers to observe a class, educators can gain fresh perspectives on their teaching methods. Peer observers can offer constructive feedback, highlighting strengths and areas for improvement. In turn, observing others also allows educators to learn new strategies or techniques, creating a culture of shared learning and mutual development.

c. Video Recordings of Lessons

Recording lessons and reviewing them is a powerful way to reflect on teaching practices. Unlike memory or perceptions, videos provide an accurate account of the classroom environment, teacher-student interactions, and teaching methods. By watching recorded lessons, educators can objectively evaluate their performance, paying attention to body language, tone, classroom management, and student engagement. This technique offers the opportunity to see the classroom from a student's perspective, helping teachers identify areas they might have otherwise overlooked.

d. Engaging in Reflective Discussions

Reflective discussions, either in formal settings like professional development groups or informally with colleagues, offer teachers an opportunity to share experiences and insights. These discussions encourage collaborative reflection, where educators can pose questions, challenge assumptions, and develop new ideas. Group reflection helps expand individual perspectives, making it a powerful tool for professional growth.

e. Surveys and Feedback from Students

Students are valuable stakeholders in the teaching process, and their feedback can provide critical insights into the effectiveness of teaching strategies. By using surveys or informal feedback sessions, educators can gauge students' understanding, engagement, and learning experiences. This technique ensures that teaching is student-centered, focusing on their needs and adjusting practices accordingly.

Strategies to Implement Reflective Teaching

To ensure that reflective teaching becomes an integral part of a teacher's practice, the following strategies can be employed:

a. Set Clear Reflection Goals

Like any other aspect of teaching, reflective practices should have clear goals. Educators must identify the areas they wish to reflect upon, whether it's lesson planning, student behavior, or teaching methods. Defining specific goals ensures that reflections remain focused and productive.

b. Use Structured Reflection Models

Using structured reflection models like Gibbs' Reflective Cycle or Schön's Reflection-in-Action and Reflection-on-Action can provide a systematic approach to reflective teaching. These models guide teachers through a step-by-step reflection process, from describing the experience to identifying learning outcomes and future actions. Such frameworks offer clarity and direction, making reflection a more intentional practice.

c. Time Management and Scheduling Reflection

One of the major challenges teachers face is finding the time for reflection amidst their demanding schedules. To overcome this, educators can schedule reflection sessions as part of their regular routine. Setting aside a few minutes at the end of each day or week ensures that reflection becomes a habit rather than a sporadic task.

d. Professional Development Workshops

Participating in professional development workshops that focus on reflective teaching practices can help educators learn new strategies and tools for self-evaluation. Workshops offer an opportunity to engage with experts and peers, sharing insights and learning from others' experiences. These sessions often introduce educators to new reflective techniques that can enhance their teaching practice.

e. Embrace Continuous Learning

Reflective teaching is rooted in the belief that learning is an ongoing process, not just for students but for educators as well. Teachers who actively seek out new knowledge, stay updated with the latest educational trends, and adopt new teaching techniques demonstrate a growth mindset. Continuous professional development and a willingness to experiment with new strategies are essential components of reflective teaching.

Benefits of Reflective Teaching

a. Professional Growth and Development

Reflective teaching enables educators to become more self-aware, recognizing their strengths and identifying areas for improvement. By continuously analyzing and adapting their teaching methods, teachers can enhance their skills and stay abreast of best practices. This leads to improved professional competence and greater confidence in their teaching abilities.

b. Improved Student Outcomes

A teacher who engages in reflective practice is more likely to be in tune with students' needs. Reflection allows educators to identify learning gaps, assess the effectiveness of their instructional methods, and make adjustments as needed. As a result, students benefit from a more personalized and adaptive learning experience, leading to better academic performance and increased engagement.

c. Enhanced Classroom Environment

Reflective teaching fosters a positive classroom environment where students feel heard, valued, and supported. Teachers who reflect on their communication styles and classroom management techniques can create an atmosphere that encourages open dialogue, mutual respect, and collaborative learning.

d. Adaptability and Flexibility

Teachers who engage in reflective practice become more adaptable and flexible in their approaches. They are better equipped to handle challenges and make real-time adjustments to their lessons based on the needs of their students. This flexibility enhances the learning experience and fosters a more responsive and dynamic classroom environment.

Challenges in Reflective Teaching

While reflective teaching offers numerous benefits, it is not without its challenges. Educators may face difficulties such as time constraints, lack of support, or the discomfort of critically analyzing their own performance. Moreover, without a structured approach, reflections may become superficial or inconsistent, limiting their effectiveness. To overcome these challenges, schools and educational institutions should provide teachers with the necessary resources, time, and support to engage in meaningful reflective practices.

Conclusion

Reflective teaching is an essential practice for educators who seek to continuously improve their teaching methods and enhance student learning. By employing techniques such as journaling, peer observation, video recordings, and engaging in reflective discussions, teachers can gain valuable insights into their classroom practices. The strategies outlined, such as setting clear reflection goals, using structured reflection models, and managing time effectively, ensure that reflection becomes an integral part of teaching practice. Despite the challenges, the benefits of reflective teaching—increased professional growth, improved student outcomes, and a more adaptive classroom environment—are well worth the effort. As education continues to evolve, reflective teaching remains a vital tool for creating effective, student-centered learning experiences.

FIVE

Chapter 5: Developing Critical Reflection Skills

"The only sustainable competitive advantage is an organization's ability to learn faster than the competition.":Peter Senge.

Critical reflection is a vital skill in education, fostering deep understanding and enabling individuals to evaluate their experiences, beliefs, and practices. This chapter explores the essence of critical reflection, its significance in personal and professional development, and strategies to cultivate these skills. By engaging in critical reflection, educators can enhance their teaching practices, promote lifelong learning, and empower students to become reflective thinkers.

Understanding Critical Reflection

Critical reflection goes beyond simple introspection; it involves analyzing experiences to uncover deeper meanings and implications. According to Dewey (1933), reflection is a "systematic, rigorous, and disciplined way of thinking" that encourages individuals to connect theory with practice. It involves questioning assumptions, considering alternative perspectives, and recognizing biases. This process is crucial in educational settings, as it helps educators evaluate their teaching methods, adapt to diverse learning needs, and improve student outcomes.

Importance of Critical Reflection

The significance of critical reflection in education can be summarized in several key points:

Enhancing Teaching Practices: Critical reflection allows educators to assess the effectiveness of their teaching methods. By analyzing what worked and what didn't, they can make informed adjustments to improve student engagement and learning.

Promoting Lifelong Learning: Developing critical reflection skills fosters a mindset of continuous improvement. Educators who engage in reflective practice are more likely to seek professional development opportunities, keeping their knowledge and skills up to date.

Empowering Students: Encouraging students to engage in critical reflection helps them take ownership of their learning. It enables them to analyze their progress, identify strengths and weaknesses, and set meaningful goals.

Supporting Diversity and Inclusion: Critical reflection encourages educators to consider diverse perspectives and adapt their teaching to meet the needs of all students. This inclusivity fosters a supportive learning environment where every student can thrive.

Strategies for Developing Critical Reflection Skills

To cultivate critical reflection skills, educators can employ various strategies that promote thoughtful analysis and evaluation of experiences.

Journaling

Journaling is a powerful tool for fostering critical reflection. Educators can maintain reflective journals to document their thoughts, experiences, and insights. Regularly writing about teaching practices encourages self-examination and helps identify patterns in behavior and decision-making. Prompts such as "What went well today?" and "What could I improve?" can guide the journaling process, prompting deeper reflection.

Peer Collaboration

Collaborative reflection with peers can enhance the reflective process. Educators can engage in discussions about their teaching experiences, sharing successes and challenges. This exchange of ideas allows for different perspectives, encouraging critical thinking and leading to innovative solutions. Professional learning communities (PLCs) can serve as a platform for such collaborative reflection, fostering a culture of continuous improvement.

Critical Incident Analysis

Analyzing critical incidents—specific events that significantly impacted teaching or learning—can deepen reflective practice. Educators can select incidents that evoke strong emotions or raise questions about their practices. By examining these incidents through a structured framework, such as Gibbs' Reflective Cycle, educators can identify the underlying causes and explore alternative approaches.

Incorporating Feedback

Feedback from students, colleagues, and mentors is invaluable for critical reflection. Educators should actively seek feedback on their teaching methods and be open to constructive criticism. Analyzing feedback helps educators recognize areas for improvement and validate effective practices. Implementing changes based on feedback demonstrates a commitment to growth and enhances the learning experience for students.

Engaging with Theoretical Frameworks

Familiarizing oneself with educational theories and frameworks can enrich the reflective process. By connecting experiences with established theories, educators can gain deeper insights into their practices. For example, exploring Kolb's Experiential Learning Theory can help educators understand how their experiences influence learning outcomes. This theoretical lens can guide reflective discussions and enhance the understanding of teaching and learning dynamics.

Challenges in Developing Critical Reflection Skills

While the benefits of critical reflection are clear, educators may encounter challenges in developing these skills. Some common obstacles include:

Time Constraints

The demands of teaching often leave little time for reflection. Educators may feel overwhelmed by administrative tasks, lesson planning, and student assessments, making it difficult to prioritize reflective practices. To address this, schools can encourage a culture of reflection by allocating time for educators to engage in reflective activities.

Resistance to Change

Some educators may resist critical reflection due to fear of criticism or discomfort with change. They may be accustomed to traditional teaching methods and reluctant to question their practices. Building a supportive community that values reflection and professional growth can help alleviate these fears and encourage educators to embrace new approaches.

Lack of Training

Many educators may not receive formal training in reflective practices. Providing professional development opportunities focused on critical reflection can equip educators with the necessary skills and tools. Workshops, seminars, and online courses can introduce educators to reflective frameworks and strategies, promoting a culture of critical inquiry.

Conclusion

Developing critical reflection skills is essential for educators seeking to enhance their teaching practices and promote student success. By engaging in reflective activities such as journaling, peer collaboration, and critical incident analysis, educators can gain valuable insights into their experiences. Despite the challenges, cultivating critical reflection is a worthwhile endeavor that fosters a culture of continuous improvement and empowers both educators and students. Ultimately, critical reflection is not just a skill; it is a mindset that nurtures lifelong learning and fosters a deeper understanding of the teaching and learning process.

SIX

Chapter 6: Reflective Teaching in Classroom Practice

"Reflection turns experience into insight."— John Dewey

Reflective teaching is an essential aspect of the educational process that promotes continuous improvement and professional growth for educators. It is a practice rooted in critical self-reflection that encourages teachers to examine their teaching methods, understand their students' learning processes, and enhance the overall educational experience. In this essay, we will explore the concept of reflective teaching, its significance in classroom practice, the strategies that can be employed to implement it effectively, and its impact on both teachers and students.

Understanding Reflective Teaching

Reflective teaching involves a systematic approach where educators critically analyze their teaching experiences to gain insights into their practice. This process entails evaluating one's teaching methods, student interactions, and the overall learning environment. Reflective teaching is based on the premise that teaching is not just about delivering content; it also involves understanding how students learn, what motivates them, and how to create a conducive learning environment.

According to Schön (1983), reflection can be categorized into two types: reflection-in-action and reflection-on-action. Reflection-in-action occurs during the teaching process, where educators make immediate adjustments based on the classroom dynamics and student responses. In contrast, reflection-on-action happens after the teaching session, where educators assess their performance, analyze what worked, what didn't, and how they can improve in the future. Both forms of reflection are crucial for professional development and can significantly enhance teaching efficacy.

Significance of Reflective Teaching

Enhancing Teacher Effectiveness

Reflective teaching allows educators to critically evaluate their teaching practices, leading to enhanced effectiveness. By reflecting on their instructional strategies, teachers can identify areas of strength and areas that require improvement. This self-awareness fosters a growth mindset, encouraging teachers to adapt their methodologies to meet the diverse needs of their students. For instance, a teacher may realize that certain teaching strategies are not resonating with their students and may decide to explore alternative approaches, such as differentiated instruction or project-based learning.

Promoting Student Engagement and Learning

When teachers engage in reflective practice, they become more attuned to their students' needs, preferences, and learning styles. This awareness enables educators to tailor their teaching methods to foster greater student engagement and facilitate deeper learning. Reflective teaching encourages educators to seek student feedback, assess student understanding, and create a classroom environment where students feel valued and motivated to participate actively.

For instance, a reflective teacher may use formative assessments to gauge student understanding and adjust their instruction accordingly.

Fostering a Collaborative Learning Environment

Reflective teaching can foster collaboration among educators, creating a culture of shared learning and professional growth. When teachers engage in reflective practice, they often share their experiences, insights, and strategies with their colleagues, promoting a collaborative environment. This collaboration can take various forms, such as peer observations, team teaching, and professional learning communities. Through these collaborative efforts, educators can support each other in their reflective journeys, leading to improved teaching practices and student outcomes.

Contributing to Professional Development

Reflective teaching serves as a foundation for ongoing professional development. Educators who engage in reflective practice are more likely to pursue opportunities for growth, such as attending workshops, enrolling in courses, or seeking mentorship. This commitment to continuous learning not only benefits the individual teacher but also positively impacts the entire educational institution. Schools that prioritize reflective teaching create a culture of lifelong learning, where educators are empowered to develop their skills and adapt to the ever-changing educational landscape.

Strategies for Implementing Reflective Teaching

Journaling and Self-Assessment

One effective strategy for reflective teaching is maintaining a reflective journal. Educators can document their teaching experiences, thoughts, and observations in a journal, allowing them to reflect on their practice regularly. This process encourages self-assessment and critical thinking, as teachers analyze their successes and challenges. Journaling also serves as a valuable resource for future reference, enabling educators to track their progress over time.

Peer Observations and Feedback

Collaborating with colleagues through peer observations can significantly enhance reflective teaching. Teachers can observe each other's classrooms, providing constructive feedback and sharing best practices. This process fosters a culture of openness and support, allowing educators to learn from one another's experiences. Feedback from peers can offer fresh perspectives and highlight areas for improvement that may have gone unnoticed.

Professional Learning Communities (PLCs)

Engaging in Professional Learning Communities (PLCs) is another effective strategy for reflective teaching. PLCs consist of groups of educators who collaborate to discuss instructional practices, share resources, and engage in collective reflection. These communities provide a supportive environment where educators can share their challenges and successes, facilitating professional growth and fostering a sense of belonging. PLCs can focus on specific topics, such as technology integration, differentiated instruction, or assessment practices, allowing educators to deepen their understanding of relevant issues.

Student Feedback and Assessments

Incorporating student feedback into the reflective teaching process is essential. Educators can use surveys, interviews, or informal discussions to gather insights from their students regarding their learning experiences. Understanding students' perspectives can help teachers identify areas for improvement and tailor their instruction to better meet students' needs. Additionally, using formative assessments allows educators to gauge student understanding and adjust their teaching strategies accordingly.

Video Reflection

Utilizing video recordings of classroom sessions can provide educators with a powerful tool for reflection. By reviewing videos of their teaching, educators can analyze their instructional practices, observe student engagement, and identify areas for improvement. This process allows for a more objective evaluation of teaching methods and can lead to actionable insights for enhancing classroom practice.

Challenges of Reflective Teaching

Despite its numerous benefits, reflective teaching is not without challenges. Some educators may find it difficult to allocate time for reflection amid the demands of teaching. Additionally, the process of self-reflection can be uncomfortable, as it requires educators to confront their weaknesses and acknowledge areas where they may need to grow. Furthermore, a lack of administrative support or a school culture that does not prioritize reflective practice can hinder teachers' ability to engage in meaningful reflection.

To overcome these challenges, educational institutions should create a supportive environment that encourages reflective practice. Providing designated time for reflection, offering professional development opportunities focused on reflection, and fostering a culture of collaboration can empower educators to engage in reflective teaching more effectively.

Conclusion

Reflective teaching is a vital component of effective classroom practice that promotes professional growth, enhances teacher effectiveness, and fosters a positive learning environment for students. By engaging in reflective practices such as journaling, peer observations, and seeking student feedback, educators can gain valuable insights into their teaching methods and make informed decisions that benefit their students. Despite the challenges associated with reflective teaching, its significance in shaping effective educators cannot be overstated. As the educational landscape continues to evolve, reflective teaching will remain an essential practice that empowers educators to adapt, grow, and ultimately enhance the learning experiences of their students.

SEVEN

Chapter 7: Pedagogical Skills Improvement through Reflection

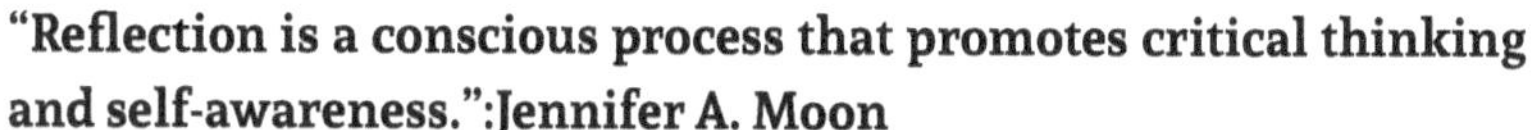

"Reflection is a conscious process that promotes critical thinking and self-awareness.":Jennifer A. Moon

Reflection is an essential component of professional development for educators, particularly in enhancing pedagogical skills. It serves as a powerful tool for self-assessment, enabling teachers to critically evaluate their practices, understand their students better, and adapt their teaching methods accordingly. This chapter explores the role of reflection in improving pedagogical skills, emphasizing its importance in fostering effective teaching and learning environments.

The Concept of Reflection in Education

Reflection, in the educational context, refers to the process of critically examining one's own teaching practices and experiences. It involves analyzing what worked well, what didn't, and why certain strategies were effective or ineffective. Reflective practice encourages educators to think deeply about their teaching methods, student engagement, and the overall learning environment. This process not only helps in identifying areas for improvement but also promotes a mindset of continuous learning and adaptation.

The Benefits of Reflective Practice

Enhanced Self-Awareness: One of the primary benefits of reflective practice is the development of self-awareness among educators. By regularly reflecting on their teaching practices, educators can identify their strengths and weaknesses, leading to a better understanding of their instructional style and effectiveness. This awareness is crucial for making informed decisions about future teaching strategies.

Informed Decision-Making: Reflective practice enables educators to make informed decisions based on their observations and experiences. By analyzing past lessons and student interactions, teachers can modify their approaches to better meet the needs of their students. This data-driven decision-making process fosters a more personalized and effective learning experience.

Improved Student Engagement: Reflective practices can lead to increased student engagement. When educators reflect on their teaching, they are more likely to consider student feedback, learning preferences, and interests. This responsiveness helps create a more inclusive and engaging classroom environment, ultimately enhancing student motivation and learning outcomes.

Professional Growth: Continuous reflection contributes to professional growth and development. Educators who engage in reflective practice are more likely to seek out professional development opportunities, collaborate with peers, and stay updated on best practices in pedagogy. This commitment to growth enhances their overall effectiveness as educators.

Strategies for Implementing Reflective Practice

To reap the benefits of reflective practice, educators can employ various strategies:

Journaling: Maintaining a reflective journal is one of the most effective methods for documenting thoughts, experiences, and insights related to teaching. Educators can write about their daily experiences, challenges faced, and successful strategies implemented in the classroom. Regular journaling promotes a habit of reflection and serves as a valuable resource for future reference.

Peer Observation and Feedback: Collaborating with colleagues through peer observation is another effective strategy for reflective practice. Educators can observe each other's teaching and provide constructive feedback. This practice not only fosters a culture of collaboration but also exposes educators to different teaching styles and techniques.

Video Analysis: Recording classroom sessions and reviewing them later allows educators to observe their teaching from an objective perspective. Analyzing video recordings can reveal insights about student interactions, instructional delivery, and classroom management. This method encourages educators to critically evaluate their practices and identify areas for improvement.

Professional Learning Communities (PLCs): Participating in PLCs provides educators with opportunities to engage in collaborative reflection. These communities foster a culture of sharing experiences, discussing challenges, and brainstorming solutions. The collective insights gained from these discussions can lead to improved pedagogical practices.

Self-Assessment Tools: Utilizing self-assessment tools, such as rubrics or checklists, can guide educators in evaluating their teaching practices. These tools encourage critical thinking about specific aspects of teaching, helping educators identify strengths and areas for growth.

Overcoming Barriers to Reflection

Despite the benefits of reflective practice, some educators may face barriers to implementation:

Time Constraints: Many educators struggle to find time for reflection amidst their busy schedules. To overcome this barrier, schools and institutions can prioritize reflective practice by allocating specific time for teachers to engage in reflective activities.

Lack of Support: Educators may feel unsupported in their reflective efforts. Creating a supportive culture within schools, where reflection is encouraged and valued, can help educators feel more comfortable engaging in reflective practices.

Fear of Judgment: Some educators may hesitate to reflect openly due to fear of judgment from peers or superiors. Fostering an environment where constructive feedback is valued and where mistakes are seen as learning opportunities can alleviate this fear.

The Impact of Reflection on Student Outcomes

Research has shown that reflective practice not only enhances educators' pedagogical skills but also positively impacts student outcomes. Educators who engage in reflection tend to create more student-centered learning environments, leading to higher levels of student engagement, motivation, and achievement. When teachers adapt their practices based on reflective insights, students benefit from more tailored instruction that meets their individual needs.

Moreover, reflective educators are better equipped to foster critical thinking and problem-solving skills among their students. By modeling reflective practices, teachers encourage students to engage in their own reflection, promoting a culture of continuous learning within the classroom.

Conclusion

In conclusion, reflective practice is a vital component of improving pedagogical skills in education. It empowers educators to critically evaluate their teaching, make informed decisions, and continuously adapt their practices to meet the diverse needs of their students. By embracing reflection, educators not only enhance their professional growth but also create more effective and engaging learning environments. As the educational landscape continues to evolve, reflective practice will remain an essential tool for fostering excellence in teaching and learning.

EIGHT

Chapter 8: Reflective Teaching and Technology Integration

"Technology will not replace great teachers, but technology in the hands of great teachers can be transformational." — George Couros

Reflective teaching is a crucial component of professional development for educators, emphasizing continuous improvement through self-analysis and critical thinking. As educational landscapes evolve, the integration of technology into teaching practices has become increasingly vital. This chapter explores the relationship between reflective teaching and technology integration, highlighting how reflective practices can enhance the effective use of technology in the classroom.

Understanding Reflective Teaching

Reflective teaching involves an ongoing process of self-examination, where educators assess their teaching practices, attitudes, and strategies. The concept, rooted in the work of educational theorists such as John Dewey and Donald Schön, encourages teachers to critically reflect on their experiences, decisions, and the impact of their teaching on student learning. Reflective teaching is not merely about evaluating successes and failures; it requires a deeper analysis of the underlying reasons for these outcomes. This introspective approach fosters a growth mindset, enabling educators to adapt and refine their practices.

Reflective teaching can be facilitated through various methods, such as journals, peer observations, and discussions. By engaging in reflective practices, teachers can identify strengths and areas for improvement, ultimately leading to enhanced pedagogical effectiveness. This self-awareness is crucial for adapting to the diverse needs of learners and creating an inclusive classroom environment.

The Role of Technology in Education

Technology has become an integral part of education, transforming how teachers deliver content and how students engage with learning materials. The advent of digital tools has opened up new avenues for communication, collaboration, and creativity in the classroom. From interactive whiteboards and learning management systems to mobile applications and online resources, technology offers innovative ways to enhance the learning experience.

However, the integration of technology is not without challenges. Educators must navigate issues such as digital equity, the potential for distraction, and the need for effective training. Therefore, it is essential for teachers to reflect on their technological practices to ensure that they are using these tools purposefully and effectively. Reflective teaching provides a framework for evaluating technology integration, enabling educators to consider how technology enhances or hinders the learning process.

Connecting Reflective Teaching with Technology Integration

The intersection of reflective teaching and technology integration offers several benefits for educators. First, reflective practices encourage teachers to assess the relevance and effectiveness of the technology they use. This assessment is vital in ensuring that technological tools align with educational goals and meet the needs of diverse learners. For example, a teacher may implement a new educational app in the classroom. Through reflection, the educator can evaluate whether the app supports student engagement, promotes critical thinking, and facilitates collaborative learning. If the app does not meet these criteria, the teacher can seek alternatives or adjust their approach.

Second, reflective teaching fosters a culture of experimentation and innovation. When teachers are encouraged to reflect on their practices, they are more likely to explore new technologies and instructional strategies. This willingness to experiment can lead to the discovery of tools that enhance student learning outcomes. For instance, a teacher might experiment with flipped classroom models, utilizing video lessons to free up class time for collaborative activities. By reflecting on the outcomes of this approach, the educator can refine their implementation and share successful strategies with colleagues.

Furthermore, reflective teaching can enhance professional development regarding technology integration. Educators who engage in reflective practices are better equipped to identify their learning needs and seek relevant training opportunities. This proactive approach to professional growth ensures that teachers stay updated on emerging technologies and best practices in digital pedagogy. Professional learning communities can serve as platforms for sharing experiences, discussing challenges, and collaboratively developing solutions for effective technology integration.

Challenges of Reflective Teaching and Technology Integration

Despite the advantages, several challenges may arise when attempting to integrate reflective teaching and technology. Time constraints in the curriculum can limit opportunities for reflection, as teachers often juggle numerous responsibilities. Additionally, the fast-paced nature of technological advancements can make it challenging for educators to keep up with new tools and their potential applications in the classroom.

Moreover, not all educators may feel comfortable with technology, leading to resistance in integrating these tools into their teaching. This discomfort can stem from a lack of training, fear of failure, or uncertainty about how to effectively use technology in their pedagogical practices. Addressing these challenges requires a supportive environment that encourages risk-taking, collaboration, and ongoing professional development.

Strategies for Effective Reflection and Technology Integration

To effectively integrate reflective teaching and technology, educators can employ several strategies:

Create Reflective Journals: Encourage teachers to maintain reflective journals where they document their experiences with technology integration. This practice allows educators to track their growth, identify successful strategies, and recognize areas for improvement.

Engage in Peer Observations: Establish a culture of peer observations, where teachers can observe each other's practices. This collaborative approach fosters constructive feedback and shared learning experiences.

Participate in Professional Learning Communities: Form professional learning communities focused on technology integration. These groups can provide a space for educators to share resources, discuss challenges, and celebrate successes.

Utilize Technology for Reflection: Leverage digital tools, such as video recordings or online discussion forums, to facilitate reflection. For example, educators can record their lessons and review them to identify areas for improvement.

Set Specific Goals: Encourage teachers to set specific goals related to technology integration and reflective practices. These goals can provide direction and motivation for ongoing professional development.

Conclusion

Reflective teaching and technology integration are intertwined aspects of effective pedagogy. By engaging in reflective practices, educators can critically assess their use of technology and adapt their approaches to meet the needs of their students. This dynamic relationship fosters a culture of continuous improvement, encouraging educators to explore innovative strategies that enhance learning experiences. As technology continues to evolve, reflective teaching will remain essential for navigating the complexities of modern education, ensuring that teaching practices remain relevant, effective, and inclusive. Ultimately, the integration of reflective teaching and technology can lead to transformative educational experiences that empower both educators and learners.

NINE

Chapter 9: Reflective Teaching for Lifelong Learning

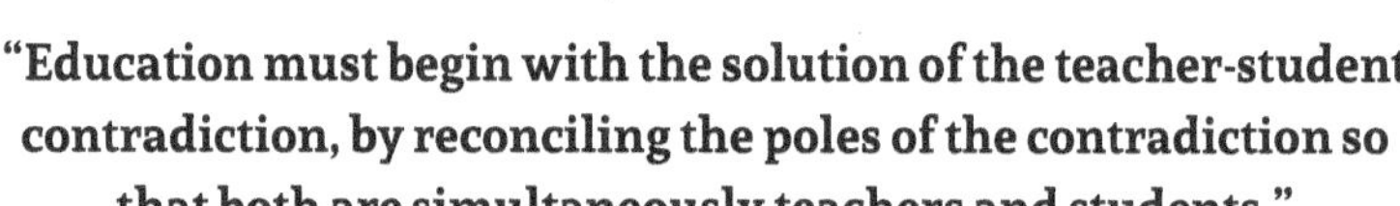

"Education must begin with the solution of the teacher-student contradiction, by reconciling the poles of the contradiction so that both are simultaneously teachers and students."
– Paulo Freire, Brazilian educator and philosopher.

Reflective teaching is a dynamic and conscious process where educators engage in critical self-assessment and introspection to improve their teaching methods and student learning outcomes. It goes beyond the routine execution of lessons, involving thoughtful consideration of what happens in the classroom, why it happens, and how it can be refined. This concept aligns with lifelong learning, as reflective teaching encourages teachers to continuously learn and adapt, fostering both professional growth and improved educational outcomes for students.

The Concept of Reflective Teaching

At its core, reflective teaching is about educators critically analyzing their instructional practices, identifying areas for improvement, and actively seeking ways to enhance their effectiveness. This approach empowers teachers to be proactive, rather than reactive, in addressing classroom challenges. Reflective teaching is rooted in the belief that teaching is not a static profession; rather, it is an evolving practice that benefits from continuous self-evaluation and adaptation.

The practice of reflective teaching can take many forms. Teachers may reflect individually, through journaling or self-assessment, or collaboratively, by engaging in peer observations, discussions, and feedback sessions with colleagues. This reflective process allows teachers to view their practice from multiple perspectives, enabling them to consider various factors that influence teaching and learning, such as student needs, classroom dynamics, instructional strategies, and the broader educational context.

Key Elements of Reflective Teaching

Several key elements contribute to the effectiveness of reflective teaching. These include:

Self-awareness: Reflective teachers develop a keen awareness of their strengths and weaknesses in the classroom. This involves recognizing one's teaching style, identifying areas that may need improvement, and understanding how personal beliefs, biases, and attitudes can affect teaching practices and student outcomes.

Critical thinking: Reflective teaching requires teachers to think critically about their actions, decisions, and the impact these have on student learning. This involves questioning assumptions, analyzing the effectiveness of instructional strategies, and exploring alternative approaches that may lead to better results.

Feedback and collaboration: Reflection is enriched through feedback from students, peers, and mentors. Engaging in collaborative discussions with colleagues provides opportunities for shared learning and professional development. Constructive feedback helps teachers identify blind spots, refine their practices, and build a community of reflective practitioners.

Continuous improvement: Reflective teaching is an ongoing process. It is not about reaching a final destination but rather about continuously striving to improve. Teachers who embrace reflective practices are committed to lifelong learning and professional growth. They are open to experimenting with new techniques, assessing their effectiveness, and making necessary adjustments.

Benefits of Reflective Teaching

Reflective teaching offers numerous benefits for both educators and students. For teachers, it promotes professional growth by fostering a mindset of lifelong learning. Through reflection, teachers gain a deeper understanding of their practice and develop the ability to make informed, intentional decisions about their teaching strategies. This leads to more effective instruction, greater job satisfaction, and a stronger sense of professional identity.

For students, reflective teaching creates a more responsive and adaptive learning environment. Teachers who reflect on their practice are better equipped to meet the diverse needs of their students, adjust their methods to suit different learning styles, and create an inclusive, supportive classroom atmosphere. As a result, students are more likely to feel engaged, motivated, and empowered to succeed.

Reflective Teaching as a Pathway to Lifelong Learning

The connection between reflective teaching and lifelong learning is clear. Lifelong learning refers to the continuous pursuit of knowledge and skills throughout an individual's life. In the context of education, lifelong learning involves teachers staying updated with new pedagogical theories, educational technologies, and best practices to remain effective in their roles.

Reflective teaching fosters lifelong learning by encouraging educators to view their professional development as a continuous journey. It challenges teachers to stay curious, open-minded, and willing to adapt to new educational paradigms. As education evolves, so must teachers, and reflective practices serve as a critical tool for navigating this ever-changing landscape.

Moreover, reflective teaching aligns with the principles of experiential learning, where teachers learn through experience, reflection, and adaptation. By analyzing their classroom experiences and applying insights gained through reflection, teachers engage in a cycle of continuous improvement that mirrors the process of lifelong learning. This not only enhances their professional skills but also models the value of lifelong learning for their students.

Strategies for Implementing Reflective Teaching

Implementing reflective teaching in daily practice requires intentional effort and the use of specific strategies. Some effective methods include:

Keeping a teaching journal: Writing regularly about classroom experiences, successes, and challenges provides a structured way for teachers to reflect on their practice. Journals allow teachers to document their thoughts, analyze what worked and what didn't, and track their professional growth over time.

Conducting self-assessment: Self-assessment tools, such as rubrics or checklists, can help teachers evaluate their performance in specific areas, such as lesson planning, classroom management, or student engagement. This helps in identifying areas where improvement is needed and setting goals for future development.

Seeking peer observations: Inviting colleagues to observe lessons and provide feedback is an effective way to gain new perspectives on teaching practices. Peer observations allow teachers to receive constructive criticism, share ideas, and collaborate on solutions to common challenges.

Engaging in professional learning communities (PLCs): PLCs offer a platform for teachers to come together, share their experiences, and engage in collective reflection. These communities foster a culture of collaboration and mutual support, helping teachers learn from each other and stay informed about new developments in education.

Using student feedback: Soliciting feedback from students provides valuable insights into how teaching practices are perceived from the learners‘ perspective. Students can offer feedback on teaching methods, classroom dynamics, and the effectiveness of instruction. This feedback can inform teachers’ reflections and guide their efforts to enhance student learning.

Setting professional development goals: Teachers who engage in reflective practice are more likely to set meaningful professional development goals. These goals may involve learning new instructional strategies, improving classroom management techniques, or exploring emerging technologies in education. By setting and pursuing these goals, teachers can stay motivated and committed to their lifelong learning journey.

Challenges in Reflective Teaching

While reflective teaching has many benefits, it is not without challenges. One common obstacle is time. Teachers often face demanding schedules, leaving little time for deep reflection. Additionally, the emotional nature of reflection, especially when confronting areas of weakness, can be difficult for some educators. Overcoming these challenges requires a commitment to prioritizing reflection and seeking support from colleagues and administrators.

Another challenge is the tendency for reflection to become superficial. For reflection to be truly effective, it must go beyond surface-level observations and delve into deeper analysis of teaching practices and their impact. Teachers must be willing to engage in honest self-assessment and be open to feedback from others.

Conclusion

Reflective teaching is a powerful approach that fosters both professional growth and enhanced student learning. By engaging in continuous self-assessment, seeking feedback, and collaborating with colleagues, teachers can refine their instructional practices and adapt to the changing demands of education. Reflective teaching is inherently linked to lifelong learning, as it encourages educators to remain curious, adaptable, and committed to their professional development. Through reflective practice, teachers not only improve their own effectiveness but also contribute to a culture of lifelong learning within their schools and communities. In this way, reflective teaching serves as a critical tool for educators seeking to make a lasting impact on their students and their profession.

TEN

Chapter 10: Case Studies and Practical Applications

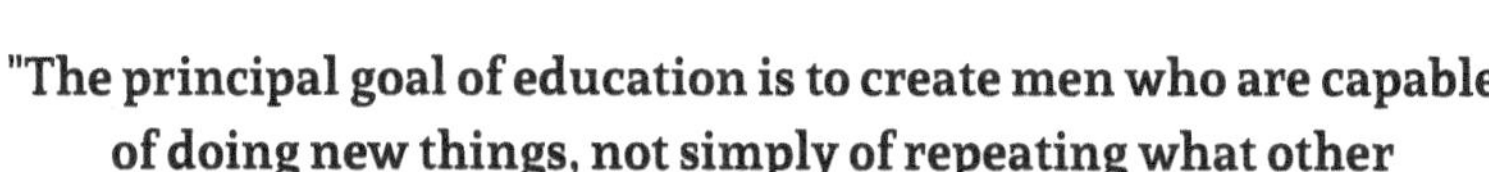

"The principal goal of education is to create men who are capable of doing new things, not simply of repeating what other generations have done."-Jean Piaget

The integration of case studies and practical applications in English pedagogy plays a crucial role in bridging the gap between theoretical knowledge and real-world teaching practices. This approach not only provides a deeper understanding of pedagogical theories but also equips educators with the skills and strategies necessary for addressing diverse classroom challenges. Chapter 10 delves into the importance of case studies and practical applications, highlighting their impact on improving instructional methods, fostering student engagement, and promoting reflective teaching practices. Through real-life examples, this chapter emphasizes how effective pedagogy is built upon continuous adaptation to the evolving needs of learners.

The Role of Case Studies in English Pedagogy

Case studies in education are detailed accounts of real or hypothetical classroom situations that provide teachers and students with the opportunity to analyze and solve problems. They often present scenarios that highlight challenges teachers may face in diverse educational settings, such as classroom management, lesson planning, differentiated instruction, or addressing the needs of students with varying abilities.

In English pedagogy, case studies allow teachers to explore how different teaching methodologies work in practice. For example, a case study might describe a classroom where students struggle with language acquisition. By analyzing the teacher's approach, such as incorporating differentiated learning techniques, peer tutoring, or scaffolding, educators can gain insights into how these strategies may work in their own classrooms.

One notable case study could involve the teaching of Shakespeare to high school students with mixed language abilities. The challenge for the teacher is to make the dense, archaic language of Shakespeare accessible to both native English speakers and ESL (English as a Second Language) students. Through this case study, educators can evaluate different instructional strategies, such as using visual aids, modern translations, or role-playing activities, to make the text more relatable and understandable.

By engaging with such case studies, teachers can reflect on their teaching practices, think critically about the effectiveness of different approaches, and apply the lessons learned to improve their instruction. This form of reflective practice helps teachers adapt their teaching to better meet the needs of their students, fostering a more inclusive and effective learning environment.

Practical Applications in English Teaching

Practical applications in English pedagogy refer to the use of hands-on, experiential learning strategies that teachers implement to enhance their instructional practices. These strategies are grounded in real-life scenarios and are aimed at improving students' language proficiency, comprehension, and communication skills.

One key aspect of practical applications in English teaching is the incorporation of technology. In today's digital age, teachers have access to a variety of technological tools that can enrich the learning experience. For example, using educational apps and online platforms, such as language learning games, interactive grammar exercises, and virtual storytelling, can make learning more engaging and effective for students.

In a case where students are learning English vocabulary and grammar, practical applications could include using mobile apps that offer gamified quizzes or flashcards, enabling students to practice language skills in a fun and interactive manner. This use of technology not only caters to the digital literacy of modern learners but also enhances motivation and retention, as students engage with the content on a deeper level.

Another significant practical application in English pedagogy is collaborative learning. Group activities such as peer editing, group discussions, and cooperative writing projects allow students to engage in meaningful communication, helping them develop critical thinking and teamwork skills. For instance a teacher could assign a group project where students collaboratively create a short story, with each member contributing different parts of the narrative. This activity not only improves language skills but also fosters creativity and teamwork.

Furthermore, drama-based activities serve as a powerful practical application in English teaching. Role-playing, dramatization, and simulations allow students to immerse themselves in the language in a more dynamic and engaging way. For instance, a teacher might assign students different characters from a novel or a play, and ask them to perform key scenes. This helps students develop not only their language skills but also their confidence and public speaking abilities.

Benefits of Integrating Case Studies and Practical Applications

The integration of case studies and practical applications into English pedagogy offers numerous benefits for both teachers and students. First, it enhances critical thinking and problem-solving skills. By analyzing case studies, teachers can think through complex pedagogical problems, consider multiple perspectives, and make informed decisions that are grounded in evidence-based practices.

For students, case studies and practical applications bring learning to life. Rather than passively absorbing information, students engage with the material, apply their knowledge in meaningful ways, and see the relevance of what they are learning. This active involvement fosters a deeper understanding of the subject matter and increases student engagement.

Additionally, practical applications provide opportunities for students to practice language skills in real-world contexts. Whether through group discussions, presentations, or creative writing projects, students learn to apply the rules of grammar, syntax, and vocabulary in authentic communication situations. This hands-on approach is particularly beneficial for ESL students, who may struggle with language acquisition in traditional lecture-based settings.

Moreover, these methods promote reflective teaching practices. Teachers who regularly engage with case studies and practical applications are more likely to reflect on their own teaching methods and identify areas for improvement. This reflective practice encourages a mindset of continuous learning and professional development, ultimately leading to better teaching outcomes.

Challenges and Considerations

While the use of case studies and practical applications offers many advantages, there are also challenges to consider. One common issue is the time and effort required to implement these methods effectively. Designing meaningful case studies, planning collaborative activities, and integrating technology into the classroom all require careful preparation and a willingness to adapt.

Another challenge is ensuring that case studies and practical applications are accessible to all students. In a diverse classroom, students may have varying levels of language proficiency, learning styles, and needs. Teachers must be mindful of these differences and provide appropriate scaffolding and support to ensure that all students can participate and benefit from these approaches.

Finally, teachers must balance the use of case studies and practical applications with other instructional methods. While these strategies are valuable, they should not replace traditional teaching methods entirely. Instead, they should complement other forms of instruction, creating a well-rounded and comprehensive approach to English pedagogy.

Conclusion

Chapter 10 emphasizes the transformative potential of case studies and practical applications in English pedagogy. These methods empower teachers to think critically about their instructional practices, adapt to the needs of their students, and create engaging and meaningful learning experiences. By incorporating real-life scenarios and hands-on activities into the classroom, educators can enhance student learning, promote language proficiency, and foster a more dynamic and inclusive learning environment. Ultimately, the effective use of case studies and practical applications is key to preparing students for success in both academic and real-world communication.

ELEVEN

Chapter 11: Future Directions of Reflective Teaching

"Critical reflection involves a critique of the presuppositions on which our beliefs have been built."
-Stephen D. Brookfield:

Reflective teaching has long been a cornerstone of effective educational practice, providing teachers with a structured method for assessing their own approaches and the impact they have on student learning. As education continues to evolve, so too must the practice of reflective teaching. Future directions in reflective teaching will likely be shaped by technological advancements, changing educational needs, and a growing focus on diversity, inclusivity, and mental well-being. In this essay, we will explore some key trends that are set to shape the future of reflective teaching, including the role of technology, the shift toward student-centered learning, and the increasing focus on teacher well-being.

Integration of Technology in Reflective Practice

One of the most significant future directions for reflective teaching is the integration of technology. Digital tools, such as e-portfolios, video recordings, and online reflection platforms, allow teachers to document and analyze their teaching practices more effectively. For instance, teachers can record their lessons and use the footage to analyze their performance, identify areas for improvement, and reflect on how they engage with students. Such tools offer greater objectivity than traditional reflective methods, which rely on memory and subjective accounts.

Moreover, artificial intelligence (AI) and machine learning are likely to play a greater role in reflective teaching. AI can provide personalized feedback to teachers based on data analysis, helping them pinpoint specific areas for development. For example, an AI-driven platform could analyze student engagement and participation in real-time, offering insights into which teaching strategies are most effective for different groups of learners. This level of granular feedback, combined with the teacher's own reflections, can lead to more targeted professional growth.

Additionally, online communities and collaborative platforms are becoming central to reflective practice. Teachers can engage in collaborative reflection with colleagues from around the world, share best practices, and offer constructive feedback through digital platforms. This global perspective enriches the reflective process, fostering professional development across different educational systems and contexts.

Student-Centered Reflective Teaching

Another future direction in reflective teaching is the shift from teacher-centered to student-centered reflection. Traditionally, reflective teaching has focused on the teacher's actions, decisions, and strategies. However, future approaches will likely emphasize the student's learning experience as the focal point of reflection. Teachers will reflect on how their instructional practices impact students' engagement, motivation, and understanding.

This shift aligns with the growing emphasis on personalized and differentiated instruction, where teaching is adapted to meet the individual needs of students. Reflective teachers will increasingly need to assess how well they are supporting diverse learners, including students with different learning styles, cultural backgrounds, and levels of ability. For example, teachers might reflect on how effectively they integrate multimodal learning resources to accommodate visual, auditory, and kinesthetic learners.

Student feedback will also play a more prominent role in reflective teaching. Future educators are likely to involve students in the reflection process, gathering their insights on the learning experience. This could be done through surveys, interviews, or informal discussions. By incorporating student voices into reflection, teachers can gain a deeper understanding of the impact of their teaching and make adjustments based on actual learner feedback.

Reflective Teaching and Inclusivity

Inclusivity will be a critical area of focus for reflective teaching in the future. As classrooms become more diverse, with students of different racial, cultural, linguistic, and socio-economic backgrounds, teachers will need to reflect on how inclusive their practices are. This means critically assessing whether their teaching methods, materials, and classroom environments are accessible and welcoming to all students, especially those from marginalized or underrepresented groups.

Future reflective practices will likely include an emphasis on culturally responsive teaching, where teachers reflect on how their own biases and assumptions may influence their interactions with students. Reflective teachers will need to assess whether they are creating equitable learning opportunities for all students and fostering a classroom culture that values diversity. This process may involve reflecting on how to incorporate diverse perspectives into the curriculum, adapt teaching strategies to support English language learners, and ensure that all students feel valued and respected in the classroom.

Teachers will also need to reflect on how well they are promoting inclusivity beyond the academic curriculum, such as in their interactions with students and in the social dynamics of the classroom. For instance, reflective teachers might consider how they can better support students' mental health and emotional well-being, creating a safe and supportive learning environment for all.

Emphasis on Teacher Well-being

In the future, reflective teaching will increasingly focus on the well-being of teachers themselves. The teaching profession can be stressful, with high demands and often limited resources. Burnout is a growing concern, and reflective practice may serve as a tool for teachers to manage their mental and emotional health.

Reflecting on personal well-being and self-care strategies will become an integral part of professional growth. Teachers will be encouraged to reflect on their work-life balance, stress levels, and overall job satisfaction. By identifying the sources of stress and burnout, teachers can develop strategies to cope with these challenges and maintain a healthier mindset.

Additionally, institutional support for reflective teaching may expand, with schools and educational organizations providing resources for professional reflection that includes mental health support. Reflective practices will no longer be limited to pedagogy and curriculum but will encompass teachers' emotional well-being, allowing for a more holistic approach to professional development.

Collaborative Reflective Teaching

Collaboration is another key trend that will shape the future of reflective teaching. While reflection has traditionally been an individual practice, there is increasing recognition of the value of collaborative reflection. Teachers working in teams can share experiences, provide mutual support, and learn from each other's successes and challenges.

Professional learning communities (PLCs) and peer-coaching models are likely to become more prevalent in schools. In these settings, teachers engage in regular reflective discussions with their peers, examining specific aspects of their teaching and offering feedback. This collective reflection fosters a culture of continuous improvement, where teachers learn not only from their own experiences but also from the insights and experiences of others.

Collaborative reflection can also break down the isolation that teachers often experience in their profession, creating a supportive network that enhances both professional growth and personal well-being. In this sense, the future of reflective teaching will be more community-oriented, where shared learning and collective growth are prioritized.

Conclusion

The future of reflective teaching is set to be dynamic, shaped by technological advancements, a greater focus on inclusivity, the well-being of teachers, and the increasing emphasis on student-centered learning. As education evolves, reflective practice must also adapt, allowing teachers to critically assess and refine their approaches in a way that meets the needs of modern learners and promotes their own professional and personal growth. By embracing these future directions, educators can ensure that reflective teaching remains a powerful tool for fostering continuous improvement and creating positive learning environments for all students.

TWELVE
REFERENCES

- Schön, D. A. (1983). The Reflective Practitioner: How Professionals Think in Action. Basic Books.
- A foundational text in reflective practice, Schön explores how professionals engage in reflective thinking and develop expertise.
- Brookfield, S. D. (1995). Becoming a Critically Reflective Teacher. Jossey-Bass.
- Brookfield emphasizes the importance of reflection in teaching and provides practical strategies for teachers to develop a reflective practice.
- Korthagen, F. A., & Vasalos, A. (2005). Levels in reflection: Core reflection as a means to enhance professional growth. Teachers and Teaching, 11(1), 47-71.
- This article presents a model of core reflection to aid teachers in enhancing their pedagogical skills and professional development.
- Zeichner, K. M., & Liston, D. P. (2013). Reflective Teaching: An Introduction. Routledge.
- This book provides a comprehensive overview of reflective teaching and connects theory to practical applications in classroom practice.

- Farrell, T. S. C. (2013). Reflective Practice in ESL Teacher Development Groups: From Practices to Principles. Palgrave Macmillan.
- This book addresses reflective practice in the context of language teaching, focusing on ESL educators and offering case studies and strategies.
- Larrivee, B. (2000). Transforming teaching practice: Becoming the critically reflective teacher. Reflective Practice, 1(3), 293-307.
- Larrivee discusses the importance of critical reflection for transforming teaching practices and advancing professional growth.
- Dewey, J. (1933). How We Think: A Restatement of the Relation of Reflective Thinking to the Educative Process. Heath & Co.
- Dewey's classic work on reflective thinking and its application to education.
- Rodgers, C. (2002). Defining reflection: Another look at John Dewey and reflective thinking. Teachers College Record, 104(4), 842-866.
- Rodgers revisits Dewey's theory of reflection and its relevance for modern education.
- Shulman, L. S. (1987). Knowledge and teaching: Foundations of the new reform. Harvard Educational Review, 57(1), 1-22.
- Shulman discusses the knowledge base necessary for effective teaching, linking it to reflective practice and pedagogical development.
- Mezirow, J. (1991). Transformative Dimensions of Adult Learning. Jossey-Bass.
- Mezirow's work on transformative learning theory highlights the role of reflection in adult education and professional growth.

www.ingramcontent.com/pod-product-compliance
Lightning Source LLC
LaVergne TN
LVHW090125160826
845673LV00015B/1023
9798895887271